First published in 2003 by Miles Kelly Publishing Ltd,
Bardfield Centre, Great Bardfield, Essex, CM7 4SL

British Library Cataloguing-in-Publication Data
A catalogue record for this book is available from the British Library

ISBN 1-84236-296-8

2 4 6 8 10 9 7 5 3 1

Project Manager: Ruthie Boardman
Cover Design: Stuart Catterson
Proofreader: Jenny Rooney

Contact us by email: info@mileskelly.net
Check our website and purchase other Miles Kelly products:
www.mileskelly.net

Printed in Italy

THE WORLD'S MOST DIFFICULT MUSIC QUIZZES

Christopher Rigby

Miles Kelly PUBLISHING

About the author

Born in Blackburn, Lancashire in 1960, Christopher Rigby has been compiling and presenting pub quizzes for the past 15 years. When he is not adding to his material for quizzes, Christopher works in the car industry. He is married to Clare – they have two teenage daughters, Hollie and Ashley and share their home with two demented dogs called Vespa and Bailey. A keen Manchester United fan Christopher lists his heroes as George Best and Homer Simpson.

The World's Most Difficult Quizzes Explained

From punk to pop and from Beethoven to Blur, this quiz book comprises 90 quizzes each containing ten questions to test the expertise of even the most ardent music lover.

If you know who replaced Keith Moon in The Who or the name of the priest in the Beatles hit 'Eleanor Rigby' then this is the book for you!

QUIZ ONE

General

1. Which musical featured the song 'If I Were a Bell'?

2. Which city witnessed the birth and death of the classical composer Schubert?

3. Which pop quintet is made up from members of the Pearson family?

4. Which chart topping pop group of the 1960s took their name from the title of a John Wayne film?

5. 'Something to Dance About' is a song that features in which musical?

6. Which pop group originally performed under the name of The Invaders?

7. Which Hollywood heart-throb is mentioned in the lyrics of the Shania Twain hit 'That Don't Impress Me Much'?

8. Victor Willis provided lead vocals for which chart topping group of the 1970s?

9. Who was the first composer to appear on a British bank note?

10. Which singer collaborated with Cliff Richard on the hit record 'Whenever God Shines His Light'?

ANSWERS

1. *Guys And Dolls* 2. Vienna 3. Five Star 4. The Searchers 5. *Call me Madam* 6. Madness 7. Brad Pitt 8. Village People 9. Edward Elgar 10. Van Morrison

6

QUIZ TWO

Identify the singers from their real names...

1. Sean Coombs
2. Roberta Streeter
3. Charles Westover
4. Clive Powell
5. Harold Ray Ragsdale
6. Walden Robert Cassotto
7. Herbert Buckingham Khaury
8. Marvin Lee Aday
9. Vincent Damon Furnier
10. George Michael Braddock

ANSWERS

1. Puff Daddy, now known as P Diddy 2. Bobbie Gentry 3. Del Shannon
4. Georgie Fame 5. Ray Stevens 6. Bobby Darin 7. Tiny Tim 8. Meatloaf
9. Alice Cooper 10. Mickey Dolenz

QUIZ THREE

General

1. Which pop star played the manager of Whitney Houston in the film *The Bodyguard*?

2. Who composed the theme music for *Coronation Street*?

3. By what name are Carl, Dennis, Brian, Mike and Al collectively known?

4. In which Italian city are "two children begging in rags" according to the Peter Sarstedt hit 'Where do You go to my Lovely'?

5. In which film did Elvis Presley sing 'Wooden Heart'?

6. The musical *The Boys From Syracuse*, is based on which Shakespeare play?

7. Who won eight Grammy Awards for the album *Supernatural*?

8. Which New Jersey born singer sued Burt Bacharach in 1972 for breaking a contractual obligation?

9. Crispian Mills, the son of Hayley Mills, is the lead singer of which pop group?

10. Which film directed by Mike Leigh chronicled the life story of the composers Gilbert and Sullivan?

ANSWERS

1. Gary Kemp 2. Eric Spear 3. The Beach Boys 4. Naples 5. GI Blues 6. A Comedy of Errors 7. Carlos Santana 8. Dionne Warwick 9. Kula Shaker 10. Topsy Turvy

QUIZ FOUR

Singing actors

1. Which actor had a minor hit single in 1971 with the song 'The Way You Look Tonight'?

2. Which former *Eastenders* actress had a 1997 hit with the song 'Sweetness'?

3. Who links the film *Harry Potter and the Philosopher's Stone* with the hit record 'Macarthur Park'?

4. Which actor sang a duet with Barbara Streisand on the 1988 hit 'Till I Loved You'?

5. Who provided the singing voice of Jessica Rabbit in *Who Framed Roger Rabbit*?

6. The Kate Winslet hit song 'What If' featured in an animated version of which classic novel?

7. Which comedy actor hit the charts with the song 'Don't Laugh at me' in 1954?

8. Who provided backing vocals on the Laurel and Hardy hit 'The Trail of the Lonesome Pine'?

9. Which song did the cast of the film *There's Something About Mary* sing during the closing credits?

10. Who collaborated with Peter Sellers on the 1960 hit 'Goodness Gracious Me'?

ANSWERS

1. Edward Woodward 2. Michelle Gayle 3. Richard Harris 4. Don Johnson 5. Amy Irving 6. *A Christmas Carol* 7. Norman Wisdom 8. The Avalon Boys 9. 'Build Me Up Buttercup' 10. Sophia Loren

QUIZ FIVE

....

General

1. Which crooner was born Terry Parsons?

2. Which soul legend was backed by the Famous Flames?

3. Which 1950 film directed by Billy Wilder was adapted into a stage musical by Andrew Lloyd Webber?

4. Which song was inspired by the crimes of a schoolgirl called Brenda Spencer?

5. Whose autobiography is entitled *I Used to be an Animal but I'm all Right Now*?

6. Which Shakespeare play, written in 1591, became the title of a Top 10 hit in 1981?

7. In which country was the composer Chopin born?

8. Which chart topping pop group took their name from a feline in TS Eliot's *Old Possum's Book of Practical Cats*?

9. Which song contains the line, "The words of the prophet are written on the subway halls"?

10. Who had a hit record in 1987 with the theme song from the TV show *Moonlighting*?

QUIZ SIX

A round on album covers

1. Which Rod Stewart album cover shows him making a giant stride from the UK to the USA?

2. Where can Mae West, Edgar Allen Poe, Bob Dylan, Tony Curtis, Marilyn Monroe, Oscar Wilde, Sonny Liston, Lewis Carroll and Albert Einstein be seen in close proximity?

3. Which Oasis album cover features a Rolls Royce submerged in a swimming pool?

4. What kind of metallic object features on the album cover *Sticky Fingers* by the Rolling Stones?

5. What does Bruce Springsteen have in his right back pocket on the cover of *Born in the USA*?

6. What sport is depicted on the album cover of Blur's *Parklife*?

7. Which album by Pink Floyd features an inflatable pig floating over a factory on the cover?

8. Which Roxy Music album cover features Jerry Hall sprawled across a rocky coast?

9. Who connects the film *The Great Escape* and the album cover *Band on the Run*?

10. Which album cover features Elton John stepping into the mythical land of Oz?

ANSWERS

1. *Atlantic Crossing* 2. All featured on the cover of Sergeant Pepper's Lonely Hearts Club Band 3. *Be Here Now* 4. Zip 5. A red handkerchief 6. Greyhound racing 7. *Animals* 8. *Siren* 9. James Coburn 10. *Goodbye Yellowbrick Road*

QUIZ SEVEN

General

1. Which pop group named themselves after Holy Island?
2. What is the name of the villain in *The Threepenny Opera*?
3. Who was the first artist to have a posthumous No 1 hit?
4. In the 1965 film *Cat Ballou*, who sang 'The Ballad of Cat Ballou'?
5. With whom did Elton John sing a duet in the song 'Act of War'?
6. Which musical instrument has a German name which when translated into English means "bell play"?
7. In 1998 who became the oldest female singer to have a UK No 1 hit single?
8. What was the first ever song to be played on MTV?
9. What is the name of the mythical land that the Beatles sailed to in the animated film *Yellow Submarine*?
10. What do the initials RCA stand for with regard to the record label?

QUIZ EIGHT

A night at the opera

1. What is the nationality of the composer of Carmen?

2. On whose novel was the opera *Billy Budd* based?

3. Which famous opera house opened on August 3, 1778?

4. *A Knight At The Opera* is the title of the autobiography of which Welsh singer?

5. Which Gilbert & Sullivan opera is set in the Tower of London?

6. What is the world's largest opera house?

7. Which opera by Benjamin Britten features the death of a young boy on a fishing boat?

8. Which Puccini opera heroine leaps to her death from a castle in Rome?

9. "A policeman's lot is not a happy one" is a line sung in which operetta?

10. What is the occupation of the operatic character Rigoletto?

ANSWERS
1. French (Bizet) 2. Herman Melville 3. La Scala in Milan 4. Sir Geraint Evans
5. *The Yeoman of the Guard* 6. The Metropolitan Opera House in New York
7. *Peter Grimes* 8. *Tosca* 9. *The Pirates Of Penzance* 10. Jester

13

QUIZ NINE

....

General

1. After which song was Chelsea Clinton named?
2. Pete Fardon, James Honeyman Scott and Martin Chambers. Which female lead singer completes the line up of this pop group?
3. Which song from the musical *Oliver* won a Best Song Oscar?
4. Which 1996 No 1 hit shares its title with a 1961 film?
5. The song 'Everything is Coming up Roses' features in which musical?
6. Which composer was the subject of a No 1 hit in 1986 and an Oscar winning film in 1984?
7. Which pop group have had hit records singing about a famous clown, the inventor of the telephone and an American Indian chief?
8. Who narrates the best selling album *The War of the Worlds*?
9. How is the singer Helen Mitchell better known?
10. Which song was a hit for Tommy Steele and Guy Mitchell in 1957?

Melba 10. 'Singing The Blues.'
4. *Breakfast At Tiffany's* 5. *Gypsy* 6. Mozart 7. Sweet 8. Richard Burton 9. Dame Nellie
1. Chelsea Morning 2. Chrissie Hynde of The Pretenders 3. 'Consider Yourself'
ANSWERS

QUIZ TEN

A lyric round

1. What is the first country mentioned in the lyrics of the hit record 'Hit Me With Your Rhythm Stick'?

2. Which song contains the line, "The history book on the shelf is always repeating itself"?

3. Greta Garbo, Marlon Brando, Grace Kelly, Fred Astaire, Ginger Rogers and Bette Davis are all mentioned in the lyrics of which song?

4. Which song contains the line, "Buying bread from a man in Brussels"?

5. According to the lyrics of 'Don't You Want Me' where was the waitress working?

6. Which song ends with the line, "God speed your love to me"?

7. Which song contains the line, "I'm gonna hit the highway like a battering ram, on a silver black phantom bike"?

8. Which film character is described in a song as "a flibbertigibbet, a will o' the wisp, a clown"?

9. What are the last three words of the lyrics of 'Bohemian Rhapsody'?

10. What are the first three parts of the body mentioned in the Beatles song 'Hey Jude'?

ANSWERS

1. Sudan (in the deserts of Sudan) 2. 'Waterloo' 3. 'Vogue' by Madonna 4. 'Down Under' by Men At Work 5. A cocktail bar 6. 'Unchained Melody' 7. 'Bat out of Hell' 8. Maria in *The Sound of Music* 9. The wind blows 10. Heart, skin and shoulder.

QUIZ ONE

General

1. Which operetta is subtitled 'The Lass That Loved a Sailor'?
2. Which song character's stockings needed mending on a Thursday night?
3. What is the nationality of the composer Bela Bartok?
4. Which musical instrument is called a *fagotto* in Italy?
5. In which city was Gloria Estefan born?
6. Which pop group's last top 40 hit was entitled 'Do you Believe in Magic?'
7. What connects the Eurovision Song Contests of 1970, 1980, 1987, 1992, 1993, 1994 and 1996?
8. Under what name do the pop duo of Ben Watt and Tracy Thorn perform?
9. Which American teenager had a world wide No 1 in 1987 with the song 'I Think We're Alone Now'?
10. Who performed the theme for the Bond movie *Never Say Never Again*?

ANSWERS

1. HMS *Pinafore* 2. 'Lady Madonna' 3. Hungarian 4. Bassoon 5. Havana 6. Bay City Rollers 7. All won by Ireland 8. Everything but the Girl 9. Tiffany 10. Lani Hall

QUIZ TWO

Instrument information

1. The *rebec* was an early form of which instrument?

2. For which musical instrument is the prestigious annual Tchaikovsky competition held?

3. Which jazz clarinettist acquired the nickname of 'The King of Swing'?

4. On which part of the bagpipes is the melody played?

5. In which Mozart opera is the hero Tamino pursued by a dragon?

6. On which record label was the album *Tubular Bells* recorded?

7. The name of which musical instrument is derived from two Greek words meaning 'sweet tune'?

8. What nationality is Adolph Sax, the inventor of the saxophone?

9. On what is a paradiddle performed?

10. Viennese, Baroque and E flat are all types of which instrument?

ANSWERS

1. Violin 2. Piano 3. Benny Goodman 4. Chanter 5. *The Magic Flute* 6. Virgin 7. Dulcimer, from the words *dulce* and *melos* 8. Belgian 9. Drums 10. Oboe

17

QUIZ THREE

··

General

1. Asher and Waller are the surnames of which 1960s duo?
2. Which was the first Irish pop group to have five No 1 hits?
3. Which song was a hit for The Supremes in 1971 and for Bananarama in 1988?
4. What was Glenn Miller's signature tune?
5. What type of nut would you associate with the pop star born August Darnell?
6. In which pop group was Tony McCarrol replaced by Alan White in 1994?
7. Who wrote the score for the musical *A Chorus Line*?
8. What connects the songs 'Telegram Sam', 'Dance With The Devil' and 'C'mon Everybody'?
9. Catfish Row provides the setting for which opera?
10. Who is the singing sister of Loretta Lynn?

QUIZ FOUR

Under the covers

1. Who had the original hit with the song 'Tainted Love' covered by Soft Cell?

2. Which 1986 No 1 hit was covered by Steps in 2001?

3. The song 'Suspicious Minds' was covered by Gareth Gates for which animated film?

4. Who collaborated with the Beach Boys on a 1996 re-release of 'Fun, Fun, Fun'?

5. Boyzone's first No 1 single was a cover version of which 1960s hit?

6. Celine Dion charted with the song 'All by Myself'. Which singer recorded the original version in 1976?

7. Which Abba hit was covered by Blancmange in 1984?

8. Bread recorded the original version of the song 'Everything I Own'. Name the two artists who topped the charts with the song in 1964 and 1987.

9. Robbie Williams first hit as a solo artist was a cover version of which song?

10. Which song has been released by Frankie Laine, The Bachelors, David Whitfield and Robson & Jerome?

ANSWERS

1. Gloria Jones 2. 'Chain Reaction' 3. *Lilo and Stitch* 4. Status Quo 5. 'Words', originally a hit for the Bee Gees 6. Eric Carmen 7. 'The Day Before You Came' 8. Ken Boothe and Boy George 9. 'Freedom', originally a hit for George Michael 10. 'I Believe'

QUIZ FIVE

General

1. What is the nationality of Father Abraham of Smurf fame?

2. Which was the first group beginning with the letter U to have a No 1 hit?

3. How many notes are there in a double octave?

4. Which singer died when the aeroplane he was travelling in crashed into Lake Monona in Wisconsin?

5. Which group collaborated with the comedian Vic Reeves on the 1991 hit 'Dizzy'?

6. Which opera features the character of Count Danilo and Baron Zeta?

7. Which group named themselves after the man who invented the seed drill in the 18th century?

8. Who are the only pop group to have a UK hit record in every single year of the 1970s?

9. What dance is most closely associated with the singer born Ernest Evans?

10. Who wrote the Tina Turner hit 'Private Dancer'?

ANSWERS

1. Dutch 2. Unit Four Plus Two 3. 15 4. Otis Redding 5. The Wonder Stuff 6. The Merry Widow 7. Jethro Tull 8. Hot Chocolate 9. The Twist, the real name of Chubby Checker 10. Mark Knopfler

QUIZ SIX

....

What do the following musical directions signify?

1. Fortissimo
2. Largo
3. Sforzando
4. Legato
5. Doloroso
6. Pizzicato
7. Allegro
8. Diminuendo
9. Rubato
10. Crescendo

QUIZ SEVEN

General

1. Which bass player for the pop group Bros was sacked with a £1million plus payoff?

2. Which couple are seen kissing on the cover of the album *Double Fantasy*?

3. What is the name of Little Orphan Annie's guardian in the musical *Annie*?

4. Who wrote the lyrics to the best selling song of the 20th century?

5. Which group played a trio of singing nuns in a 1968 TV episode of *Tarzan*?

6. What is the name of the priest in the Beatles hit 'Eleanor Rigby'?

7. The musical *Half a Sixpence* was based on a novel by which author?

8. Name the Catalonian capital that was the subject of a hit record in 1992.

9. Who replaced Keith Moon in The Who?

10. What was the first UK No 1 hit to be sung in Spanish?

ANSWERS

1. Craig Logan 2. John Lennon and Yoko Ono 3. Daddy Warbucks 4. Bernie Taupin, for 'Candle in the Wind' 5. The Supremes 6. Father McKenzie 7. HG Wells, the novel being *Kipps* 8. Barcelona 9. Kenny Jones 10. 'Begin the Beguine' by Julio Iglesias

QUIZ EIGHT

....

Who composed the following songs?

1. 'The First Cut is the Deepest', a hit for Rod Stewart

2. 'Manic Monday', a hit for The Bangles

3. 'A Good Heart', a hit for Feargal Sharkey

4. 'Pink Cadillac', a hit for Natalie Cole

5. 'The One and Only', a hit for Chesney Hawkes

6. 'Anyone who had a Heart', a hit for Cilla Black

7. 'All the Young Dudes', a hit for Mott the Hoople

8. 'It Ain't Necessarily So', a hit for Bronski Beat

9. 'Every Time we say Goodbye', a hit for Simply Red

10. 'Only Women Bleed', a hit for Julie Covington

ANSWERS

1. Cat Stevens 2. Prince 3. Maria McKee 4. Bruce Springsteen 5. Nik Kershaw 6. Burt Bacharach & Hal David 7. David Bowie 8. George Gershwin 9. Cole Porter 10. Alice Cooper

23

QUIZ NINE

General

1. How old was Buddy Holly when he died?

2. Which singer provided the female vocals on the Tears For Fears hit 'Woman In Chains'?

3. The pop star Seal was born in London in 1963. What is Seal short for?

4. Who wrote The Monkees hit record 'I'm a Believer'?

5. What connects No 1 hits by The Marcels, Danny Williams and Creedence Clearwater Revival?

6. How are the duo of Daniel Jones and Darren Hayes collectively known?

7. What is the connection between The Proclaimers and Alistair Cooke?

8. Who has had hit records singing about Claudette, Cathy, Lucille and Suzie?

9. What did Paul McCartney wear on his feet on the *Abbey Road* album cover?

10. What connects the songs 'Unchained Melody', 'Love is in the Air' and 'Everything Must Change'?

QUIZ TEN

Group therapy

1. From where did the pop group Texas take their name?
2. Which group recorded the No 1 album *Colour by Numbers*?
3. Which Swedish chart toppers comprise the Berggren family and Ulf Ekberg?
4. Which American group recorded the soundtrack for the sci-fi film *Dune*?
5. Whom did Sid Vicious replace in The Sex Pistols?
6. Which pop group established the Brother Record Label?
7. Which Scottish pop group includes husband and wife Ricky Ross and Lorraine McIntosh in their line up?
8. Who provides lead vocals for Mungo Jerry?
9. Which was the first American girl group to top the UK singles charts twice?
10. Which group topped the album charts with 'Sparkle in the Rain'?

QUIZ ONE

....

General

1. Which pop song did the Labour Party use as their theme in the 1997 General Election campaign?

2. Who died in April 1984 and was awarded a posthumous Grammy Lifetime Achievement Award 12 years later?

3. Which rocker opened the Philadelphia concert in the US version of Live Aid in 1985?

4. Which song was a hit for The Tokens in the 1960s and for Tight Fit in the 1980s?

5. Which American vocalist had hit records with the songs 'Lydia' and 'Lucky Stars'?

6. In 1988, Wembley Stadium hosted a tribute concert to celebrate whose 70th birthday?

7. Peter Wolf provides lead vocals for which US pop group?

8. Which public school was attended by the founder members of Genesis?

9. The singing of which Christmas carol provokes Ebenezer Scrooge into grabbing a ruler and threatening the singer?

10. Which song marked the chart debut of Status Quo?

ANSWERS

1.'Things Can Only Get Better' by D: Ream 2. Marvin Gaye 3. Bryan Adams 4.'The Lion Sleeps Tonight' 5. Dean Friedman 6. Nelson Mandela 7. J.Geils Band 8. Charterhouse 9.'God Rest Ye Merry Gentlemen' 10.'Pictures of Matchstick Men'

QUIZ TWO

Musicals

1. A lawyer by the name of Billy Flynn is a character in which musical?

2. On whose novel was the musical *Les Miserables* based?

3. The songs 'This Time Next Year' and 'The Greatest Star of all' feature in which musical?

4. On which Shakespeare play was the musical *Kiss Me Kate based*?

5. What is the name of the cat who sings the song 'Memory' in *Cats*?

6. Who wrote the music for the musical *Hello Dolly*?

7. Andrew Lloyd Webber and Ben Elton collaborated on which musical that centres around the sport of football?

8. Which musical features a mean spirited matron called Agatha Hannigan?

9. In which musical does Kim fall in love with Chris?

10. Which Andrew Lloyd Webber musical is based on a novel by Mary Hayley Bell?

QUIZ THREE

General

1. Which rock star died on November 22, 1997?

2. Under what name did Hilary Lefter perform on a 1982 No 1 hit?

3. On which island was the singer Nana Mouskouri born?

4. Who recorded the album *God's Great Banana Skin*?

5. The song 'Do You Know Where You're Going to' is the theme for which film?

6. How many quavers are there in a semi-breve?

7. LeAnn Rimes and Elvis Presley were both born in which state?

8. By what one word title is Beethoven's 3rd Symphony also known?

9. Which was the first musical that Rodgers & Hammerstein wrote together?

10. What is the title of The Troggs only No 1 hit?

QUIZ FOUR

....

The Eurovision Song Contest

1. Which future superstar sang, 'Ne Partez Pas Sans Moi' in The Eurovision Song Contest?

2. Who were the only UK winners of the contest in the 1990s?

3. Which country staged the first ever contest?

4. In what year was the Eurovision Song Contest first held?

5. What song did The Shadows sing in the 1975 contest?

6. What song did the transsexual Dana International sing when winning the contest?

7. Who sang the UK entry 'One Step Out of Time' in 1992?

8. What song was sung by The New Seekers in the 1972 contest?

9. Which nation did The Olsen Brothers represent in winning the song contest in 2000?

10. In which year did the contest end in a four-way tie that included Lulu amongst its winners?

QUIZ FIVE

General

1. By what six-letter name is the rap star, born Ivor Artis Jnr, better known?

2. What is the surname of the brothers who founded the pop group Right Said Fred?

3. What is the real name of the controversial rap artist Eminem?

4. The Doors took their name from the title of a book by which author?

5. Which musical features the song 'Luck be a Lady'?

6. Which 1960s pop star was backed by The Shondells?

7. Which opera singer acquired the nickname of the 'Swedish Nightingale'?

8. Which family group recorded the album *In Blue* in 2000?

9. The composers Verdi and Rossini both wrote operas based on which Shakespeare play?

10. With which musical instrument is Sonny Rollins most closely associated?

ANSWERS
1. Coolio 2. Fairbrass 3. Marshall Mathers III 4. Aldous Huxley, the novel *The Doors of Perception* 5. *Guys and Dolls* 6. Tommy James 7. Jenny Lind 8. The Corrs 9. *Othello* 10. Saxophone

QUIZ SIX

Classical

1. In which city was Johannes Brahms born?
2. What is the more popular title of Haydn's Symphony No 94?
3. Which Finish composer's works include *Finlandia*?
4. Which composer graduated from St Michael's School in 1702 to become violinist for the Chamber Orchestra of Duke Ernst of Weimar?
5. The film 'Song Without End' chronicles the life of which composer?
6. By what title is Tchaikovsky's 6th Symphony also known?
7. Name the composer of *The Rite of Spring* who died in 1971?
8. In which capital city did Claude Debussy die?
9. Who composed the 20th century opera *The Golden Cockerel*?
10. Which Russian born composer wrote his last major work entitled *Rhapsody on a Theme of Paganini* in 1934?

ANSWERS
1. Hamburg 2. 'The Surprise Symphony' 3. Jean Sibelius 4. Johann Sebastian Bach
5. Franz Liszt 6. 'The Pathetique' 7. Igor Stravinsky 8. Paris 9. Rimsky-Korsakov
10. Sergei Rachmaninov

QUIZ SEVEN

General

1. What is the last name of the pop sensation Anastacia?
2. Which composer's piece 'Adagio for Strings' featured in the Vietnam War film *Platoon*?
3. In which song did Bono sign a duet with Frank Sinatra in 1993?
4. Which film star was the subject of the biggest hit for the pop duo Haysi Fantayzee?
5. Who replaced Siobhan Fahey in Bananarama?
6. Which New York born guitarist was backed by The Rebels?
7. In which city was the singer Bjork born?
8. Which New York born singer won a Grammy award for Best New Artist in 1999?
9. For how many weeks did the song 'Love is all Around' top the UK singles charts in 1994?
10. Which Clint Eastwood film featured the song 'The First Time Ever I Saw Your Face'?

ANSWERS

1. Newkirk 2. Samuel Barber 3. 'I've Got You Under My Skin' 4. John Wayne, the song 'John Wayne Is Big Leggy' 5. Jacqui O'Sullivan 6. Duane Eddy 7. Reykjavik 8. Christina Aguilera 9. 15 weeks 10. *Play Misty for me*

QUIZ EIGHT

Tribute tunes

1. The 1975 hit 'Black Superman' by Johnny Wakelin is a tribute to which famous man?

2. Which Fascist leader is the subject of the Elvis Costello song 'Less Than Zero'?

3. Which song by Eric Clapton, a tribute to his deceased son, won a Best Record Grammy award in 1992?

4. Who is the subject of the 1945 song 'Nancy with the Laughing Eyes'?

5. Which song did Joe Cocker record as a tribute to Rita Coolidge?

6. Name the Dutch singer who recorded the song 'I Remember Elvis Presley', shortly after the death of Elvis.

7. Which frontman of The Ram Jam Band was the subject of Dexy's Midnight Runners first chart topping single?

8. Which 1970 hit was a tribute to the 16th President of the USA, the youngest winner of the Nobel Peace Prize and the 35th President of the USA?

9. The lyric, "Shadows on the hills, sketch the trees and the daffodils", features in a song that is a tribute to whom?

10. Which 1980s group released the song 'When Smokey Sings' as a tribute to Smokey Robinson?

QUIZ NINE

General

1. Which famous Australian song was based on a poem by Banjo Patterson?
2. With whom did Julio Iglesias sing a duet on the 1988 hit 'My Love'?
3. Which pop duo recorded the 1988 album *Introspective*?
4. Which musical features the song 'You Gotta Have a Gimmick'?
5. What is the nationality of the chart topping disco group Black Box?
6. Which 1962 instrumental hit was inspired by a weather satellite?
7. Located in the Appalachian Mountains what provided the title of a hit record for Lonnie Donegan in 1957?
8. With which band did Jim Diamond have a hit with the song 'I Won't Let You Down'?
9. 'Maggie May' was the first No 1 hit for Rod Stewart. What was his second?
10. What did East 17 change their name to when they attempted a comeback in 1998?

QUIZ TEN

In which country were the following composers born?

1. Alexander Borodin
2. Gustav Holst
3. Franz Liszt
4. Edvard Grieg
5. Franz Schubert
6. Antonin Dvorak
7. Felix Mendelssohn
8. Niccolo Paganini
9. Paul Dukas
10. Stephen Sondheim

ANSWERS
1. Russia 2. England 3. Hungary 4. Norway 5. Austria
6. Czechoslovakia 7. Germany 8. Italy 9. France 10. USA

SESSION 4

QUIZ ONE

General

1. Which of the Spice Girls was born in Watford in 1972?

2. Which member of Bob Marley's backing group The Wailers was shot dead by burglars?

3. Under what name did the pop group The B 52s record the song 'Meet the Flintstones'?

4. What is the alternative name for Chopin's Prelude No 15 in D Flat, Opus 28?

5. Which song provided the first UK chart hit for The Bee Gees?

6. What is the name of the doctor who is credited with the invention of the LP record?

7. Who provides lead vocals for the pop group Dawn?

8. What is the connection between the album *The Man Who* and Robert DeNiro in *Taxi Driver*?

9. Ronnie Dio and Graham Bonnet have both provided lead vocals for which rock group?

10. Which building provided the title of the biggest hit record for The New Vaudeville Band?

QUIZ TWO

A weather report

1. Who wrote the lyrics for the song 'Raindrops Keep Falling on my Head'?

2. Which song contains the line, "In the chilly hours and minutes of uncertainty, I want to be in the warm hold of your loving mind"?

3. For which group does Ian Broudie provide lead vocals?

4. Which musical features the songs 'Fit as a Fiddle' and 'Beautiful Girl'?

5. The song 'Baby It's Cold Outside' featured in which 1949 musical?

6. Which group founded in 1970 recorded the albums *Millennium* and *Raise*?

7. Who was Barbara Streisand playing on film when she sang 'Don't Rain on my Parade'?

8. Which pop group had a 1978 hit with the song 'I Can't Stand the Rain'?

9. Roy Carter, Keith Wilder, Johnny Wilder, Rod Temperton and Eric Johns have all been members of which disco group?

10. What is the English translation of the opera *Der Sturm*?

ANSWERS

1. Hal David 2. 'Catch the Wind' 3. The Lightning Seeds 4. *Singing in the Rain*
5. *Neptune's Daughter* 6. Earth, Wind and Fire 7. Fanny Brice 8. Eruption 9. Heatwave
10. The Tempest

QUIZ THREE

General

1. Lockit is the name of the gaoler in which opera?

2. What was the name of the female member of The Thompson Twins?

3. Lene Nystrom provides the lead vocals for which chart topping group?

4. What is the connection between Thor Heyerdahl and The Shadows?

5. In which European capital city was the opera *Don Giovanni* first performed?

6. What musical instrument is known as, "the clown of the orchestra"?

7. At what age did Jimi Hendrix, Jim Morrison and Janis Joplin all die?

8. In which state were the Beach Boys formed?

9. Which singer has had hits collaborating with Chris Rea, The Propellerheads and Yello?

10. What is the nationality of the chart topping singer Boris Gardner?

QUIZ FOUR

The Fab Four

1. What was the title of The Beatles first top 10 hit?

2. At which American venue did The Beatles perform their final public concert in 1966?

3. Which original member of The Beatles was born in the city of Madras?

4. Who contributed the guitar solo to the George Harrison penned song 'While my Guitar Gently Weeps'?

5. Which song provided The Beatles with their first hit in the USA?

6. Which record label turned down The Beatles in 1962 after claiming guitar groups were dead?

7. Other than The Beatles, who were are the only two pop stars who feature on the Sergeant Peppers album cover?

8. Who directed the film *A Hard Day's Night?*

9. Which female singer did The Beatles support on their first national UK tour?

10. On which TV programme did The Beatles make their first national TV appearance in 1963?

ANSWERS

1. 'Please Please Me' 2. Candlestick Park in San Francisco 3. Pete Best 4. Eric Clapton 5. 'I Want to Hold Your Hand' 6. Decca 7. Bob Dylan and Dion 8. Richard Lester 9. Helen Shapiro 10. *Thank Your Lucky Stars*

QUIZ FIVE

General

1. Who performed in the title role of *The Fresh Prince* in his early chart career and went on to become a major box office star?

2. In which city were the Four Tops formed?

3. Who sang a duet with Billy Preston on the hit record 'With you I'm Born Again'?

4. In which American state was Britney Spears born?

5. On which record label did The Spice Girls record their No 1 hits?

6. Which group's debut single 'People Need Love', reached No 17 in the Swedish singles charts?

7. Which protest singer founded the organisation Humanitas International Human Rights Committee?

8. Which song provided Elton John with his first solo No 1 in the USA?

9. Which pop group were originally called History of Headaches?

10. Which rock star took his four-letter name from a hearing aid store?

ANSWERS

1. Will Smith 2. Detroit 3. Syreeta 4. Louisiana 5. Virgin 6. Abba 7. Joan Baez 8. 'Crocodile Rock' 9. Tears For Fears 10. Bono, from a Dublin store called Bonovox

QUIZ SIX

....

What's in a name?

1. Which rock group took their name from a character in *David Copperfield*?

2. Which group who had a hit with the song 'More than I can Bear' named themselves after a tin of paint?

3. The singer Johann Holzel had a worldwide chart topping hit in 1986. Under what 5 letter name did he perform?

4. Which pop star was born William Johnson?

5. Which pop group named themselves after the Arabic word for black?

6. Right Said Fred named themselves after a 1962 hit by which comedy actor?

7. The Bay City Rollers took their name from a town in which US state?

8. Which group named themselves after the Gaelic word for family?

9. Which group founded in Illinois founded in 1968 took their name from an antique fire engine?

10. Which singer was born Pauline Matthews in 1947?

QUIZ SEVEN

General

1. Which instrumental hit that first charted in 1961 was originally titled 'Jenny'?
2. In which Gilbert & Sullivan opera is Mabel the love of Frederic?
3. Which chart topping singer appeared in the films *McVicar* and *Stardust*?
4. Which song provided James Brown with his only top 10 hit in the UK?
5. Which American band are fronted by the sister Ann and Nancy Wilson?
6. Which former 1960s pop star went on to manage Jimi Hendrix and Slade?
7. Who banged the drums for the pop group Culture Club?
8. Which singer provided lead vocals for The Crusaders hit 'Street Life'?
9. Who was born Ronald Wycherley in 1941 and died of heart disease in 1983?
10. Which song was a hit for Lipps Inc in 1980 and Pseudo Echo in 1987?

ANSWERS
1. 'Stranger on the Shore' 2. *The Pirates of Penzance* 3. Adam Faith
4. 'Living in America' 5. Heart 6. Chas Chandler 7. Jon Moss 8. Randy Crawford
9. Billy Fury 10. 'Funky Town'

QUIZ EIGHT

Can you identify the girl groups and boy bands from their line ups?

1. Kevin Scott, Kev Richardson, Nick Carter, Alexander McLean and Howie D.

2. Vernie Bennett, Kell Bryan and Easther Bennett.

3. Mark Read, Ben Adams, Christian Ingebrigtsen and Paul Marazzi.

4. Cheryl, Nadine, Kimberley, Nicola and Sarah

5. Lance Bass, JC Chasez, Joey Fatone, Chris Kirkpatrick and Justin Timberlake.

6. Lee Brennan, Jimmy Constable and Simon Dawbarn

7. Ant, Ryan, Duncan and Simon

8. Terry Ellis, Maxine Jones, Cindy Herron and Dawn Robinson

9. Adam Horovitz, Adam Yauch and Michael Diamond.

10. Nathan Morris, Wanya Morris, Shawn Stockman and Michael McCary

ANSWERS
1. The Backstreet Boys 2. Eternal 3. A1 4. Girls Aloud 5. N'Sync 6. 911 7. Blue 8. En Vogue 9. The Beastie Boys 10. Boyz II Men

QUIZ NINE

General

1. Which opera by Puccini features a chief of police called Scarpia?
2. What were Gary Puckett's backing group The Union Gap named after?
3. What was the first Beatles song that the Fab Four released on their own Apple record label?
4. What is the bestselling song to have featured in the stage musical *Whistle Down The Wind*?
5. Which pop group were formed from the remnants of Joy Division?
6. What did The Elgins rename themselves in 1961?
7. Robert Davies, the co-writer of the Kylie Minogue hit 'I Can't Get you out of my Head', was a member of which 1970s glam rock group?
8. Colin Hay provided lead vocals for which Australian pop group?
9. Which duo wrote the musical score for *Gigi*?
10. Bobby Farrell was the only male member of which chart topping act?

QUIZ TEN

....

Music at the movies

1. A milkman called Tevye is the main character in which musical?

2. On whose novel was the film *South Pacific* set?

3. Who played the Baroness, the fiancée of Captain Von Trapp in *The Sound Of Music*?

4. What is the surname of the brothers in the musical *Seven Brides For Seven Brothers*?

5. Which film featured the songs 'Sweet Home Chicago' and 'Minnie The Moocher'?

6. Which Disney animated film featured the songs 'Two Worlds' and 'Trashin' The Camp'?

7. Which song and dance man was portrayed by James Cagney in *Yankee Doodle Dandy*?

8. Who played the role of Leroy in the 1980 film *Fame*?

9. A funeral director called Mr Sowerberry features in which award winning musical?

10. What is the title of the piece of music used as the theme for *The Deer Hunter*?

QUIZ ONE

General

1. Which ballet by Aaron Copland tells the story of an American outlaw of the Wild West?

2. What is the connection between The Human League, ABC and Def Leppard?

3. Which singer is portrayed by Jessica Lange in the film *Sweet Dreams*?

4. For which 1980s band did Steve Norman play the saxophone?

5. Kylie Minogue sang 'Tears on my Pillow' on the soundtrack of which film?

6. Rita Ray was the female member of which doo-wop vocal group?

7. In which country was Lonnie Donegan born?

8. Which American singer was the first female solo artist to top the UK album charts?

9. Which composer opened the Abbey Road Record Studios in 1931?

10. Who replaced Eric Clapton in The Yardbirds?

ANSWERS
1. *Billy the Kid* 2. All were formed in Sheffield 3. Patsy Cline 4. Spandau Ballet 5. *The Delinquents* 6. The Darts 7. Scotland 8. Connie Francis 9. Edward Elgar 10. Jeff Beck

QUIZ TWO

Identify the albums from the artist
and two album tracks

1. Fleetwood Mac	'Little Lies' and 'Family Man'
2. Dire Straits	'Tunnel of Love' and 'Expresso Love'
3. Michael Jackson	'Rock with You' and 'Girlfriend'
4. The Beach Boys	'Wouldn't it be Nice' and 'Caroline'
5. The Beatles	'Taxman' and 'Doctor Robert'
6. Jason Donovan	'Sealed with a Kiss' and 'Change Your Mind'
7. REM	'Man on the Moon' and 'Everybody Hurts'
8. Genesis	'Tell me Why' and 'No Son of Mine'
9. Queen	'Fight From the Inside' and 'Spread Your Wings'
10. Boyzone	'Melting Pot' and 'Crying in the Night'

ANSWERS
1. *Tango in the Night* 2. *Making Movies* 3. *Off the Wall* 4. *Pet Sounds* 5. *Revolver*
6. *10 Good Reasons* 7. *Automatic for the People* 8. *We Can't Dance* 9. *News of the World*
10. *A Different Beat*

QUIZ THREE

General

1. Which Elvis Presley hit of 1960 was based on a Neapolitan folk song?

2. By what shorter name is Chopin's Waltz in D Flat No 1 better known?

3. Who played a student in the film *Sister Act II* and went on to record a Grammy winning album?

4. Which European principality won the Eurovision Song Contest in 1971?

5. Who backed Paul McCartney on the hit record 'We all Stand Together'?

6. What is the connection between George Williams and a 1978 No 1 hit?

7. How is Beethoven's 6th Symphony better known?

8. Under what name did the pop duo Ray Hildebrand and Jill Jackson perform in the 1960s?

9. Which popular pianist was born Trevor Stanford?

10. Under what name did Marc Almond have a hit with the song 'Black Heart'?

ANSWERS

1. 'It's Now or Never' 2. 'Minute Waltz' 3. Lauryn Hill 4. Monaco 5. The Frog Chorus'
6. George Williams was the founder of the YMCA, a No 1 for The Village People
7. 'The Pastoral' 8. Paul and Paula 9. Russ Conway 10. Marc and the Mambas

QUIZ FOUR

Identify the correct answer from the five choices given;

1. What is Mick Jagger's middle name? Paul, Phillip, Peter, Patrick or Perry

2. What is the last name of Little Eva, famed for her hit 'The Locomotion'? Barnes, Bradshaw, Billington, Boyd or Black

3. What is the name of the backing band of Jimmy James? The Vagrants, The Ventures, The Velvets, The Vipers or The Vagabonds

4. Which TV theme was composed by Danny Elfman? *The Simpsons, Cheers, Friends, Hill St Blues* or *Dr Who*

5. Which female vocal group comprised Shirley Owens Alston, Doris Kenner and Addie Harris? The Shangri-La's, The Shirelles, The Crystals, The Ronettes or The Primettes

6. In which Lancashire town were The Verve formed? Accrington, Burnley, Oldham, Wigan or Blackburn

7. On which island was Barry Gibb born? Isle of Wight, Jersey, Alderney, Guernsey or Isle of Man

8. Which group took their name from a Scritti Politti song? Wet Wet Wet, Undertones, All About Eve, Sham 69 or U2

9. Which pop legend served two years in a US jail? Sam Cooke, Jerry Lee Lewis, Chuck Berry, James Brown or Little Richard

10. Which of the following was the former name of Black Sabbath? Neptune, Earth, Venus, Saturn or Mars

QUIZ FIVE

General

1. What musical instrument was invented in the 17th century by Johann Christoph Denner?

2. Which singer was married to fellow singer James Taylor from 1972 to 1983?

3. Who was appointed violin master at Venice's La Pieta Orphanage in 1703?

4. Which former chart-topping singer ran for the Irish presidency in 1997?

5. In which decade were 45-rpm records first sold in the USA?

6. In which African country was Holly Johnson born?

7. In which city was Verdi's opera *Aida* first performed in 1871?

8. Which female singer won more Grammy Awards in the 20th century than any other woman?

9. What disease claimed the life of Frederic Chopin in 1849?

10. What is the name of the lyricist brother of George Gershwin?

QUIZ SIX

Sing a rainbow

1. Which groups debut album is entitled *Picture Book*?

2. The Pink Floyd album track 'Shine on you Crazy Diamond' is a tribute to which former band member?

3. Who replaced Ian Gillan as lead singer of Deep Purple?

4. What colour connects hit records by David Essex, Hawkwind and David Soul?

5. Which group had top 20 hits with the songs 'Badge', 'Strange Brew' and 'I Feel Free'?

6. Which David Bowie hit of 1975 was covered by Loose Ends in 1985?

7. Which song provided the pop group Christie with their only No 1 hit?

8. Under what name did Colin Vearncombe have two top 10 hits in 1987?

9. Which song was hit record for Elvis Presley, The Marcels and Showaddywaddy?

10. Which member of the 1980s pop group Orange Juice went on to have a 1990s solo hit with 'A Girl Like You'?

QUIZ SEVEN

General

1. Who composed a suite of piano pieces entitled 'Children's Corner'?

2. Which British pop star released Vida Nova in Portugal in 2002?

3. Under what name did Jonathan King record the song 'I Can't Get No Satisfaction'?

4. Which pop diva performed at the opening ceremony of the 1994 football World Cup?

5. In which group was Jay Aston replaced by Shelley Preston?

6. Who was the first British female singer to win a Grammy Award?

7. In which capital city was the singer Neneh Cherry born?

8. Name the first Scottish group to top the UK singles charts?

9. What did 'Candle in the Wind' replace as the world's best selling song?

10. Robert Smith provides lead vocals for which Goth rock giants?

ANSWERS

1. Claude Debussy 2. Cliff Richard: Vida Nova being a brand of wine from his Portuguese vineyard 3. Bubblerock 4. Diana Ross 5. Bucks Fizz 6. Petula Clark 7. Stockholm 8. Marmalade 9. 'White Christmas' 10. The Cure

QUIZ EIGHT

Which song title links each group of artists?

1. Seal, Aerosmith, Mud, Patsy Cline and Eternal

2. Michael Jackson, Carly Simon, Donny Osmond, Bronski Beat and Annie Lennox

3. Shirley Bassey, The Move, David Bowie, Kool and the Gang and New Kids on the Block

4. Paul McCartney, Petula Clark, Mary J Blige and Lionel Richie

5. Del Shannon, The Corrs, Deee-Lite, Janet Jackson and E'Voke

6. Genesis, Kim Appleby, Connie Francis, Dave Berry and The Spice Girls

7. Joan Armatrading, The Everly Brothers, Heaven 17, Wet Wet Wet and New Order

8. Rod Stewart, Madonna, Simply Red, Shaggy and Aretha Franklin

9. Chris Montez, David Bowie, Chris Rea and Five

10. Buddy Holly, Don Johnson, Ruby Murray, Jimmy Sommerville and Steps

ANSWERS
1. 'Crazy' 2. 'Why' 3. 'Tonight' 4. 'My Love' 5. 'Runaway' 6. 'Mama' 7. 'Temptation' 8. 'Angel' 9. 'Let's Dance' 10. 'Heartbeat'

QUIZ NINE

General

1. Name the three members of Duran Duran who have the surname Taylor.

2. Which was the first Liverpool group to have a No 1 hit?

3. Who has been married to members of Oasis, Simple Minds and Big Audio Dynamite?

4. Who provided the female vocals on UB40's 1985 cover version of 'I Got You Babe'?

5. Which singer formed a successful female trio with Valerie Holiday and Fayette Pinkney?

6. Which song had vocal contributions from Stevie Wonder, James Ingram, Tina Turner, Billy Joel, Lionel Richie, Willie Nelson, Michael Jackson, Diana Ross, Bob Dylan and Cyndi Lauper amongst others?

7. Whose album entitled *Brainwashed* was released posthumously in 2002?

8. Who in his teenage years was backed by a group called The Jacks?

9. What is the connection between the pop star Ringo Starr and the actor Michael Angelis?

10. In which country did the Bee Gees have their first No1 hit?

QUIZ TEN

Can you identify the artists from their only hit record and the year of its release?

1. 1968   'Simon Says'
2. 1990   'Turtle Power'
3. 1982   'I've Never Been to me'
4. 1980   'Together we are Beautiful'
5. 1984   'Big in Japan'
6. 1979   'One Day at a Time'
7. 1966   'Michelle'
8. 1976   'No Charge'
9. 1979   'Ring my Bell'
10. 1954   'Little Things Mean a Lot'

ANSWERS
1. 1910 Fruitgum Company 2. Partners In Kryme 3. Charlene 4. Fern Kinney
5. Alphaville 6. Lena Martell 7. The Overlanders 8. JJ Barrie 9. Anita Ward
10. Kitty Kallen

QUIZ ONE

General

1. Elvis Presley was buried wearing a ring that bore the inscription TCB. What do those initials stand for?

2. What is the colourful singing name of the pop star and actor born Clifford Price?

3. Which rock festival, organised by Michael Eavis, was first held on September 19, 1970?

4. What is Stevie short for in the name of Stevie Wonder?

5. Which British singer is the only recording artist to have had a hit record in the USA and UK singles charts in every single year from 1971 to 1999?

6. Who built his own recording studio called Paisley Park in Minneapolis?

7. Of which group were Gerry Rafferty and Billy Connolly both members?

8. Who released his debut album in 2002 entitled *From Now On*?

9. Which pop group fronted by Julian Cope took their name from a line in a Marvel comic featuring the superhero Daredevil?

10. Which group recorded the song 'Never Had A Dream Come True' for Children In Need?

ANSWERS

1. Taking Care of Business 2. Goldie 3. Glastonbury 4. Steveland 5. Elton John 6. Prince 7. The Humblebums 8. Will Young 9. Teardrop Explodes 10. S Club 7

QUIZ TWO

Girl power

1. In 1992 who controversially tore up a picture of the Pope on *The Saturday Night Live* TV show?

2. With which female singer did Paul Young sing a duet in the 1985 Live Aid concert?

3. Which rock star's daughter had a 2002 hit record with a cover version of the Madonna song 'Papa Don't Preach'?

4. Who was the first singer to win seven Brit Awards?

5. In which US state was singer Dolly Parton born?

6. Which Simon & Garfunkel hit was covered by The Bangles in 1988?

7. What J is the middle name of the singer Barbara Streisand?

8. Name the character played by Suzie Quatro in the sitcom *Happy Days*.

9. Whose 1983 debut solo album *She's so Unusual* earned her a Grammy Award?

10. What condiment provides the stage name of the rap star Cheryl James?

ANSWERS

1. Sinead O'Connor 2. Alison Moyet 3. Ozzy Osbourne's daughter Kelly 4. Annie Lennox 5. Tennessee 6. 'A Hazy Shade of Winter' 7. Joan 8. Leather Tuscadero 9. Cyndi Lauper 10. Salt of Salt N Pepa

QUIZ THREE

General

1. Which 1960s teen idol was born on the Isle of Wight with the name Terence Perkins?

2. Which glam rock star was born Bernard Jewry?

3. Which popular seasonal song was a hit for Bruce Springsteen in the Christmas of 1985?

4. In 1981 which family group became the first European act to win the Grand Prize at the renowned Tokyo Music Festival?

5. Which group's line up comprises of Kate Pierson, Fred Schneider, Ricky Wilson, Cindy Wilson and Keith Strickland?

6. With which group did Tom Jones collaborate on his 1988 hit 'Kiss'?

7. Which pop group starred in the 1960s film, *Catch us if you Can*?

8. Which song was a hit record for The Merseys and David Bowie?

9. Whose 1998 album entitled *R* spawned seven top 20 hits?

10. Which future singing star represented Spain in the 1970 Eurovision Song Contest?

QUIZ FOUR

....

Super macs

1. What was the name of the rock group formed by tennis stars John McEnroe and Pat Cash?

2. In the 1970s, who was backed by the Soul City Symphony?

3. Which song has been a hit for Don McLean and Roy Orbison?

4. Which film theme provided CW McCall with his only hit in 1976?

5. Which song was an unlikely hit for Patrick MacNee and Honor Blackman in 1990?

6. Which singer was 'Torn Between Two Lovers' in 1977?

7. Which composition by Paul McCartney is the world's most recorded song?

8. Which duo had a 1979 disco smash with 'Ain't no Stopping us Now'?

9. Which song was a 1974 chart topper for George McCrae?

10. Who is the lead singer of The Pogues?

QUIZ FIVE

General

1. Who has recorded hits in collaboration with Luther Vandross, Michael Jackson, Missy Elliott, Joni Mitchell and Carly Simon?

2. In which capital city was Alanis Morissette born?

3. Which incident of December 1980 is chronicled in the Mike Oldfield hit 'Moonlight Shadow'?

4. Which singing brother became a business advisor to Michael Jackson in 1987?

5. Which Billy Ocean hit featured Michael Douglas, Danny DeVito and Kathleen Turner in the video?

6. In which group did Andy Summers replace Henri Padovani?

7. Which 1995 album by Blur shares its title with a 1963 film?

8. By what four-letter name is the pop star Robert Bell better known?

9. Which singer born James Marcus Smith adopted a trouser splitting routine on stage?

10. Which pop icon was born in Lucknow, India on October 14, 1940?

QUIZ SIX

**Can you identify the songs from their lyrics? All ten
songs contain the name of an animal in the title:**

1. "Deep down in her pocket she finds 50p"

2. "Keep everything in the farmyard upset in everyway"

3. "I think I'm so sophisticated, cos I'm living my life like a good homo sapian"

4. "I may go out tomorrow if I can borrow a coat to wear."

5. "You've got your hip swinging out of bounds"

6. "The heat was hot and the ground was dry, But the air was full of sound"

7. "So unplug the jukebox and do yourself a favour"

8. "Maybe I'm just like my father, too bold"

9. "Crimson dress that clings so tight, she's out of reach and out of sight"

10. "Strut on a line its discord and rhyme, I howl and I whine I'm after you"

QUIZ SEVEN

General

1. Which rock musician was backed by the Mothers of Invention?

2. Which former assistant editor of the pop magazine *Smash Hits* enjoyed four No 1 smash hits in the 1980s?

3. Which No 1 hit was a variation of Bach's 'Suite No 3 in D major'?

4. Which song was a hit for Bobby Day and Michael Jackson?

5. Under what tasty name did the duo of Linda Green and Herbert Feemster enjoy 1970s chart success?

6. Which 1978 Kate Bush album featured the song 'Wuthering Heights'?

7. Which German band was founded by Florian Schneider and Ralf Hutter?

8. Who had a hit with the song 'Windmills of Your Mind', the theme for the film *The Thomas Crown Affair*?

9. Which actress provided lead vocals for the 1980s band Eighth Wonder?

10. The Chiffons successfully sued George Harrison after claiming that his hit 'My Sweet Lord' plagiarised which of their hit records?

QUIZ EIGHT

The answers to the following questions are all people whose surname begins with the letter M

1. Who was the first singer to have a No 1 hit in the USA and the UK?

2. The Boyzone hit 'You Needed Me' was a cover version of which Canadian singers 1978 hit?

3. Which legendary music star died in Miami on May 11, 1981?

4. Which singing sister has had hits with the songs, 'Love and Kisses', 'All I Wanna Do' and 'Jump to the Beat'?

5. Who is the lead singer of Echo and the Bunnymen?

6. Which singer changed his name to Abdul Rahman in 1998?

7. Under what name did Philip Blondheim enjoy a flower-power hit in 1967?

8. With which Italian musician did Phil Oakey collaborate on the 1984 hit 'Together in Electric Dreams'?

9. Which 1950s singing star was born Al Cernik?

10. Which soul star is backed by the Bluenotes?

QUIZ NINE

General

1. Who played the mother of Elvis Presley in the 1979 film *Elvis*?

2. With which instrument is the jazz musician King Oliver most closely associated?

3. Which duo re-formed for The Concert In Central Park in 1982?

4. Which historical event is commemorated by Tchaikovsky's '1812 Overture'?

5. Ron and Russell Mael were members of which 1970s band?

6. The rock band Steppenwolf took their name from a novel by which author?

7. Which pop trio named themselves after a pair of brothers in the *Tin Tin* cartoons?

8. Which actress provided the inspiration for the song 'Rosanna', a hit for the US group Toto?

9. In 2002 which former football manager released the single 'Its Christmas, Lets Give Love a Try'?

10. Demis Roussos and Vangelis were both members of which 1960s band?

QUIZ TEN

**Try and name the missing members
in each group of band line-ups...**

1. Alan Price, John Steel, Chas Chandler and Hilton Valentine
2. Charlie Birchill, Mike McNeil, Mel Gaynor and John Giblin
3. Scott Gorham, Brian Downey and Brian Robertson
4. Richie Sambora, David Bryan, Alec John Such and Tico Torres
5. Andy Scott, Mick Tucker and Steve Priest
6. Jimmy Destri, Chris Stein, Gary Valentine and Clem Burke
7. Tom Frazer, David Brown, Rod Harper and Gregg Rolie
8. Stuart Wood, Leslie McKeown, Alan Longmuir and Derek Longmuir
9. Graeme Clark, Neil Mitchell and Tom Cunningham
10. Charley Charles, Mickey Gallagher, Chaz Jankel, Davey Payne, John Turnbull and Norman Watt-Roy

ANSWERS

1. Eric Burdon of The Animals 2. Jim Kerr of Simple Minds 3. Phil Lynott of Thin Lizzy 4. Jon Bon Jovi of Bon Jovi 5. Brian Connolly of Sweet 6. Debbie Harry of Blondie 7. Carlos Santana of Santana 8. Eric Faulkner of The Bay City Rollers 9. Marti Pellow of Wet Wet Wet 10. Ian Dury of The Blockheads

QUIZ ONE

....

General

1. Who recorded the UK's best selling single by a female artist in 2001?

2. A brass quintet comprises of two trumpets, one trombone, one tuba and which other instrument?

3. 'Dolce Vita' in 1983 was the only hit record for which singer?

4. Stevie Wonder's Oscar winning song 'I Just Called to Say I Love You', featured in which 1984 film?

5. Which chart topping group originally performed under the name of The Nightlife Thugs?

6. In 2000 who became the first female singer to record three UK No 1 hits before her 18th birthday?

7. Which No 1 hit opens with the line, "Some people might say my life is in a rut"?

8. Which artist was the manager of the cult group Velvet Underground?

9. Under what name did Christopher Hamill sing the theme for the film *The Never Ending Story*?

10. Which chart topping cartoon group were based on comic characters created in 1942 by John Goldwater?

ANSWERS

1. Kylie Minogue with the song 'Can't Get You Out of my Head'. 2. French horn 3. Ryan Paris 4. *Woman in Red* 5. The Boomtown Rats 6. Billie Piper 7. 'Going Underground' by The Jam 8. Andy Warhol 9. Limahl 10. The Archies

QUIZ TWO

Can you answer the following questions
with 'clothing' as the clue?

1. 'Favourite Shirts' was the debut hit for which 1980s pop band?

2. Which 1960s pop group beseeched us to do the "hippy hippy shake"?

3. Nina Persson provides lead vocals for which group?

4. In 1984, who had her first hit in 25 years with the song 'Hand in Glove'?

5. Which musical features the song 'Close Every Door'?

6. Which song contains the line, "By the look in your eye I can tell you're gonna cry"?

7. How was Leo Sayer dressed when he sang 'The Show Must Go On', on his *Top Of The Pops* debut?

8. Which song topped the charts for Nancy Sinatra in 1966?

9. Who had his only Top 10 hit in 1976 with a song entitled 'Jeans on'?

10. What costume was Victor Willis known for wearing on stage?

ANSWERS

1. Haircut 100 2. The Swinging Blue Jeans 3. The Cardigans 4. Sandie Shaw
5. *Joseph and the Amazing Technicolour Dreamcoat* 6. 'Wherever I Lay my Hat That's my Home' 7. Dressed as a clown 8. 'These Boots Are Made For Walking' 9. David Dundas
10. A policeman, he was the lead singer of The Village People

QUIZ THREE

General

1. Which singer's films include *Vice Versa*, *London Town* and *Drawn Daggers*?

2. Which group took their name from a German art movement that began in 1919?

3. Which Scottish group named themselves after a song on the Steely Dan album Aja?

4. Eric Carmen's biggest solo hit 'All by Myself' was based on a melody by which classical composer?

5. What was Cliff Richard's last No 1 of the 20th century?

6. Which super group was formed in 1969 by Eric Clapton, Ginger Baker, Steve Winwood and Rick Grech?

7. Which rock giant's middle names are Robert Hayward Stenton?

8. Which Carpenters hit was a No 1 in the USA and a No 2 in the UK and was a cover version of a 1961 hit by The Marvelettes?

9. Which song has been a hit for Rick Astley, Donny Osmond and Nat King Cole?

10. Which 1960s group had the last names of Davies, Dee, Dymond, Amey and Wilson?

QUIZ FOUR

The answers to the following questions all contain the name of an animal...

1. Under what name did the duo of Gary Cooper and Michael Camacho have a 1986 hit with 'Let's Go all the Way'?

2. Which group did Kerry Katona leave to raise a family?

3. Which group embarked on their 'When Hell Freezes Over' World Tour in 1994?

4. Which group recorded the UK Christmas No 1 of 1986 with a song that was originally a hit for Isley Jasper Isley?

5. By what four-letter name is Derek Dick better known in the world of music?

6. In which pop group are the lead vocals shared by Roger Cook and Madeline Bell?

7. Name the group who charted with the song 'To Know Him is to Love Him' in 1958

8. Which pop star made a guest appearance playing Francis De Graumont in the TV series *The Equalizer*?

9. For which group does the shaven headed female singer Skin provide lead vocals?

10. Which award-winning animated pop group is drawn by the artist Jamie Hewlett and voiced by a number of real life pop stars including Damon Albarn?

ANSWERS
1. Sly Fox 2. Atomic Kitten 3. The Eagles 4. The Housemartins 5. Fish of Marillion 6. Blue Mink 7. The Teddy Bears 8. Adam Ant 9. Skunk Anansie 10. Gorillaz

QUIZ FIVE

....

General

1. What is the connection between the 1980s boy band New Edition and the film *The Bodyguard*?

2. What does MG stand for with regard to Booker T And The MGs?

3. Who connects the groups The Move, ELO and The Traveling Wilburys?

4. What was Ringo Starr's first hit as a solo artist?

5. Which British mezzo-soprano singer was created a dame in 1976?

6. Which soul star founded the Love Unlimited Orchestra?

7. What is Buddy Holly's middle name?

8. Which Glaswegian won a Grammy for Best New Artist in 1981?

9. Which film theme song contains the line, "Do not forsake me oh my darling"?

10. Which chart topping single for Chris Farlowe was written by Mick Jagger and Keith Richards?

ANSWERS

1. Bobby Brown a member of New Edition married Whitney Houston the star of the film
2. Memphis Group 3. Jeff Lynne 4. 'It Don't Come Easy' 5. Janet Baker 6. Barry White
7. Hardin 8. Sheena Easton 9. *High Noon* 10. 'Out of Time'.

70

QUIZ SIX

World music

1. In which county is the Knebworth Rock Festival held?

2. Which state mentioned in The Beatles song 'Get Back' is also the state where Linda McCartney was born?

3. In which European country is the Roskilde Rock Festival held?

4. In which country is the Delibes opera *Lakme* set?

5. Which country won the 2002 Eurovision Song Contest?

6. Which musical features the songs, 'By Strauss' and 'I'll Build A Stairway to Paradise'?

7. Which home state of Gladys Knight featured in the title of one of her hits in 1976?

8. 'High on the Rhine' is the national anthem of which country?

9. Which beach provided Barry Manilow with a world wide hit in 1978?

10. What connects the 1957 hit 'Cry Me A River', the 1989 hit 'Requiem' and the 1990 hit 'I've Been Thinking About You'?

ANSWERS
1. Hertfordshire 2. Arizona 3. Denmark 4. India 5. Latvia 6. *An American in Paris*
7. Georgia; the song 'Midnight Train To Georgia' 8. Liechtenstein 9. Copacabana
10. London; the artists Julie London, The London Boys and Londonbeat

QUIZ SEVEN

1. By what explosive name is Naomi McLean-Daley better known?

2. Who backed Sam the Sham on the song 'Wooly Bully'?

3. What 1955 film of a Broadway musical co-starred Frank Sinatra and Marlon Brando?

4. Which chart topping pop group of the 90s originally performed under the name of Joyspeed?

5. Lisa Lopez, who died in a car crash in 2002, was a member of which pop trio?

6. Which rock diva was born Patricia Andrzejewski?

7. What does the R stand for in the name of the singer R Kelly?

8. Which group formerly performed under the names of The Pendletones and Carl and The Passions?

9. What is unusual about the rock star drummer Rick Allen?

10. Which rhythm and blues legend was born Otha Ellas Bates?

QUIZ EIGHT

Can you name who sang the following seasonal hits?

1. 1983   'Cold as Christmas'
2. 1962   'Rockin' Around the Christmas Tree'
3. 1976   'Bionic Santa'
4. 1963   'All I Want for Christmas is a Beatle'
5. 1994   'All I Want For Christmas is You'
6. 1957   'Santa Bring my Baby Back to me'
7. 1967   'What Christmas Means to me'
8. 1978   'Please Come Home for Christmas'
9. 1996   'Your Christmas Wish'
10. 1992   'Christmas Through Your Eyes'

ANSWERS
1. Elton John 2. Brenda Lee 3. Chris Hill 4. Dora Bryan 5. Mariah Carey 6. Elvis Presley 7. Stevie Wonder 8. The Eagles 9. The Smurfs 10. Gloria Estefan

73

QUIZ NINE

General

1. Which Australian band originally performed under the name of The Farriss Brothers?

2. Who recorded the song 'Run Away Horses' after running away from the Go Gos?

3. For which 1985 film starring Dan Aykroyd and Chevy Chase did Paul McCartney compose and perform the theme?

4. Which hit for John Lee Hooker was used to advertise Levi Jeans?

5. What L is the middle name of Bing Crosby?

6. Under what name did Terence Lewis record the song 'Venus in Blue Jeans'?

7. With whom did Celine Dion sing a duet with in the 1997 hit 'Tell Him'?

8. To which rock star was the *Cosby Show* actress Lisa Bonet married briefly?

9. In which film did Madonna appear alongside a mountain lion?

10. Whose son recorded the album *Conscious Party* in 1988?

ANSWERS

1. INXS 2. Belinda Carlisle 3. *Spies Like us* 4.'Boom Boom' 5. Lillis, he was born Harry Lillis Crosby 6. Mark Wynter 7. Barbara Streisand 8. Lenny Kravitz 9. *Who's That Girl?* 10. Bob Marley's son Ziggy Marley

QUIZ TEN

Can you identify the songs from the following lyrics? All ten songs contain the name of an American location...

1. "Touched down in the land of delta blues, In the middle of the pouring rain"

2. "When the day is dawning on a Texas Sunday morning"

3. "When a man named Al Capone tried to make that town his own"

4. "You can be there by four thirty, cause I've made your reservation"

5. "Dearest darling, I had to write to say I won't be home anymore"

6. "All across the nation such a strange vibration"

7. "I asked my love to take a walk"

8. "Well I got down on my knees and I began to pray"

9. "These vagabond shoes are longing to stray"

10. "Tried to hitch a ride to San Francisco"

ANSWERS
1. 'Walking in Memphis' 2. 'Is This the Way to Amarillo?' 3. 'The Night Chicago Died' 4. 'Last Train to Clarksville' 5. '24 Hours From Tulsa' 6. 'San Francisco' 7. 'Banks of the Ohio' 8. 'California Dreaming' 9. 'New York, New York' 10. 'Massachusetts'.

QUIZ ONE

General

1. Which duo split in 1973 and reunited in September 1983 for a concert at the Royal Albert Hall?

2. Which rock drummer was born Colin Flooks?

3. Which former husband of Joan Collins had two No 1 hits in 1960?

4. Which chart topping single for Abba featured on the *Abbaesque* EP by Erasure?

5. Roddy Frame sang 'How Men Are' as lead vocalist for which Scottish pop group?

6. Which 1997 film featured the song 'You Sexy Thing'?

7. With which Cat Stevens song did Boyzone have a hit in 1995?

8. Which song was a No 1 hit for Elvis Presley 25 years after his death?

9. Who made his debut as conductor for the Berlin Philharmonic Orchestra in 2002?

10. Who was born Melanie Jayne Brown?

ANSWERS
1. The Everly Brothers 2. Cozy Powell 3. Anthony Newley 4. 'Take a Chance on Me' 5. Aztec Camera 6. *The Full Monty* 7. 'Father and Son' 8. 'A Little Less Conversation' 9. Sir Simon Rattle 10. Mel B of the Spice Girls

QUIZ TWO

What nationality are the following recording artists?

1. Bonnie Tyler
2. Whigfield
3. Rednex
4. Neil Young
5. 2 Unlimited
6. Ottawan
7. Vangelis
8. The Scorpions
9. Baccara
10. Jan Hammer

QUIZ THREE

General

1. Under what name was James Jewel Osterberg backed by The Stooges?

2. Michael McDonald provided lead vocals for which brotherly group?

3. What was the first Blondie album to top the charts?

4. By what much shorter name is Ian Watkins better known?

5. Who was the first David to have a No 1 hit?

6. Which pop star lost his sight at the age of seven after witnessing his brother George drown in a bathtub?

7. Which soul legend died in 1984 after lying in a coma for eight years?

8. For which TV series did Ian Dury perform the theme song 'Profoundly in Love With Pandora'?

9. Which TV series hosted by Esther Rantzen made a star of the singer Sheena Easton?

10. What is the connection between the record 'Tossing and Turning' and Harvard University?

ANSWERS

1. Iggy Pop 2. The Doobie Brothers 3. *Parallel Lines* 4. H, formerly of Steps 5. David Whitfield in 1953 with 'Answer Me' 6. Ray Charles 7. Jackie Wilson 8. *The Secret Diary of Adrian Mole* 9. *The Big Time* 10. The pop group The Ivy League performed the song and Harvard is a member of the league

QUIZ FOUR

**Try and answer the following questions –
clues can be found 'around the house'**

1. Which song was a No 1 hit for the first Norwegian group to top the UK singles charts?

2. Frankie Vaughan, Jim Lowe, Shakin' Stevens and Glen Mason have all had hits with which record?

3. What was the first hit for The Supremes following the departure of Diana Ross?

4. Which song opens with the line, "I heard you on the wireless back in '52"?

5. Which household object connects song titles by The Human League, The Beat and Pinkerton's Assorted Colours?

6. Which hit record contains the line, "We gotta install microwave ovens"?

7. Which Australian band charted in 1989 with 'Beds are Burning', a song that highlighted the persecution of Australian Aborigines?

8. Who was always in the kitchen at parties in 1980?

9. Which Oldham based group released their debut album entitled Life in 1990?

10. Which song featured with 'The Model', a double A side hit for Kraftwerk in 1981?

ANSWERS

1. A-Ha with 'The Sun Always Shines on TV'. 2. 'Green Door'. 3. 'Up The Ladder to the Roof'. 4. 'Video Killed the Radio Star'. 5. Mirror; the songs 'Mirror Man', 'Mirror in the Bathroom' and 'Mirror Mirror'. 6. Money for Nothing 7. Midnight Oil 8. Jona Lewie 9. Inspiral Carpets 10. 'Computer Love'.

QUIZ FIVE

General

1. Under what name did Graham Gouldman and Andrew Gold have a 1987 hit called 'Bridge To Your Heart'?

2. In which year was Bob Geldof awarded an honorary knighthood?

3. What was the name of the duo who were the first recording artists to have a hit with the Lennon & McCartney composition 'With A Little Help From My Friends'?

4. Which female singer's 1993 debut album is entitled *Tuesday Night Music Club*?

5. Whose hit record 'I'm Lost Without You' was played at his own funeral in 1983?

6. Which future pop star played the role of Felicity Scully in *Neighbours*?

7. Which duo recorded the album *Consequences* after leaving 10cc?

8. Which rock guitarist joined the line-up of The Eagles in 1975?

9. Which member of The Manic Street Preachers disappeared without trace in 1995?

10. Which rock and roller's backing group comprised Frannie Beecher on lead guitar, Ralph Jones on drums, Rudy Pompilli on sax and Al Pompilli on bass?

QUIZ SIX

**The answers to these ten questions are
all groups beginning with L...**

1. The Nigerian born singer Tunde Baiyewu provides lead vocals for which group?

2. What was the name of the French duo who recorded the disco smash 'Black Is Black' in 1977?

3. Which 1960s pop band took their name from a lyric in the song 'Coffee Blues' by Mississippi John Hurt?

4. Which US rock group took their name from a Jacksonville gym teacher who despised students with long hair?

5. David Hildago provided lead vocals for which chart topping group of 1987?

6. 'Einstein-A Go Go' and 'Norman Bates' were the only hit records for which 1980s group?

7. Which South African vocal group provided the backing vocals for several tracks on the Paul Simon album *Graceland*?

8. Which rock group's best selling albums include, *Houses of the Holy* and *Physical Graffiti*?

9. In the 1990s the pop group The Cast were formed from the remnants of which band?

10. Alan Hull died of heart failure in 1996. Which UK group was he the lead singer?

ANSWERS

1. Lighthouse Family 2. La Belle Epoque 3. Lovin' Spoonful 4. Lynyrd Skynyrd after the teacher Leonard Skinner 5. Los Lobos 6. Landscape 7. Ladysmith Black Mambazo 8. Led Zeppelin 9. The La's 10. Lindisfarne

QUIZ SEVEN

....

General

1. Hergest Ridge was the title of the follow up album to which 1973 best seller?

2. Tommy Lee, the estranged husband of Pamela Anderson, plays the drums for which US rock group?

3. Who was the first member of the Traveling Wilburys to die?

4. Which soul legend was shot dead on December 11, 1964?

5. Which pop star was arrested in India in 1981 after he was forced to make an unscheduled landing whilst attempting an around the world aeroplane trip?

6. Which singer acquired the nickname of Little Miss Dynamite in 1957?

7. In which city was Ozzy Osbourne born?

8. Which song was a hit for Ketty Lester in 1962 and Alison Moyet in 1987?

9. What is Sandy's last name in the film *Grease*?

10. What is Danny's last name in the film *Grease*?

ANSWERS
1. *Tubular Bells* by Mike Oldfield 2. Motley Crue 3. Roy Orbison 4. Sam Cooke 5. Gary Numan 6. Brenda Lee 7. Birmingham 8. 'Love Letters' 9. Dee 10. Zuko

QUIZ EIGHT

Cats and dogs

1. Which group had the original hit with the song 'Mama Told me Not to Come' in 1970?

2. Which film theme was a hit for Tom Jones in 1965?

3. In 1953 which female singer asked 'How Much is That Doggie in the Window'?

4. Which song opens with the line, "He painted Salford's smokey tops"?

5. Under what name did Kent LaVoie have a 1971 hit with 'Me and you and a Dog Named Boo'?

6. Which rockabilly trio comprised of Brian Setzer, Jim Phantom and Lee Rocker?

7. Who was born Steven Georgiou in 1947?

8. Which film features the song 'Everbody Wants to be a Cat'?

9. Which enduring pop group recorded the album *Dog with two Heads* in 1971?

10. What was the name of the Dutch group who had a 1976 chart topper with the song 'Mississippi'?

ANSWERS

1. Three Dog Night 2. 'What's New Pussycat' 3. Lita Roza 4. 'Matchstalk Men and Matchstalk Cats and Dogs' 5. Lobo 6. The Stray Cats 7. Cat Stevens 8. *The Aristocats* 9. Status Quo 10. Pussycat

QUIZ NINE

General

1. Jam Master Jay, shot dead in 2002, was a member of which rap group?

2. Who caused a scandal when he married his cousin Myra Gale Brown in 1957?

3. Which couple married in 1964, had a No 1 hit in 1965 and divorced in 1974?

4. Which pop star connects the films *Stormy Monday*, *Plenty* and *Lock Stock and Two Smoking Barrels*?

5. What was the title of Phil Collins first solo album?

6. Which song did Bryan Ferry record in 1981 as a tribute to John Lennon?

7. Which group was founded in 1985 by Robert Palmer, John and Andy Taylor of Duran Duran and Tony Thompson of Chic?

8. As a teenage schoolboy in 1952 who was chosen as New York City's outstanding pianist by Arthur Rubenstein?

9. What is Sade short for with regard to the singer Sade?

10. *Greetings From Asbury Park* was the 1973 debut album of which rock star?

ANSWERS
1. Run DMC 2. Jerry Lee Lewis: Myra was only 13 3. Sonny & Cher 4. Sting 5. *Face Value* 6. 'Jealous Guy' 7. The Power Station 8. Neil Sedaka 9. Folasade 10. Bruce Springsteen

QUIZ TEN

Body parts

1. Which part of the body connects the backing bands of Joan Jett and Tom Petty?

2. The theme to which Bond film was song by Sheena Easton?

3. Which Texan rock group had a hit with the song 'Legs' in 1985?

4. What part of the body connects hits by The Sutherland Brothers and The Doobie Brothers?

5. Which opera features an aria entitled 'Your Tiny Hand is Frozen'?

6. Who played Madonna's lover in the film musical *Evita*?

7. Which song pointed the way to the top of the charts for Dickie Valentine in 1954?

8. Which song contains the line, "The movement you need is on your shoulder"?

9. Which US group was founded in 1975 by David Byrne, Tina Weymouth and Chris Frantz?

10. What was Michael Jackson's last UK No 1 hit of the 20th century?

ANSWERS

1. Heart; Joan Jett and The Blackhearts and Tom Petty and The Heartbreakers 2. For Your Eyes Only 3. ZZ Top 4. Arms, Arms of Mary and Take me in Your Arms 5. La Bohème 6. Jimmy Nail 7. 'Finger of Suspicion' 8. 'Hey Jude' 9. Talking Heads 10. 'Blood on the Dancefloor.'

QUIZ ONE

General

1. Which song was a hit for Nicky Thomas in 1970 and Paul Young in 1983?

2. Which Yorkshire born rocker founded The Grease Band in 1966?

3. Gary Cherone and Nuno Bettencourt provide the vocals for which US group?

4. How are the chart topping duo of Maria Mendiola and Mayte Mateos collectively known?

5. Which pop star played a bus driver in *Spice Girls, The Movie*?

6. In Greek legend, which city was built by Amphion with the music of a lyre?

7. What does the E stand for in the name of Ben E King?

8. Daryl Dragon and Toni Tennille make up which soul duo?

9. At the age of 11 which future pop superstar played the role of Penny Gordon Woods in the US sitcom *Good Times*?

10. Which pops star's cousin Roy broke his leg in the 1959 FA Cup final?

ANSWERS

1. Love of the Common People' 2. Joe Cocker 3. Extreme 4. Baccara 5. Meatloaf 6. Thebes 7. Earl 8. Captain & Tennille 9. Janet Jackson 10. Elton John's cousin Roy Dwight

QUIZ TWO

The answer to the following questions are groups beginning with R or singers with surnames beginning with R...

1. Which group was co-founded by Chris & Eddie Amoo?

2. Which singer topped the charts with the song 'Dizzy' in 1969?

3. In 1996 which American group signed an $80 million record deal with Warner Brothers?

4. Who represented the UK in the Eurovision Song Contest in 1971 singing 'Jack in the Box'?

5. Which group had a hit with the song 'I'll be There for you', the theme music for the sitcom *Friends*?

6. Who sang a duet with Placido Domingo on the 1989 hit 'Till I Loved You'?

7. Who was made an MBE in 1980, won a Lifetime Achievement Brit Award in 1989 and received a knighthood in 1995?

8. Gwen Dickey provided lead vocals for which soul band?

9. Which was the first British group to record 30 gold albums in the USA?

10. Which Jamaican born pop star was born Rawlston Fernando Gordon?

ANSWERS
1. Real Thing 2. Tommy Roe 3. REM 4. Clodagh Rogers 5. The Rembrandts 6. Jennifer Rush 7. Cliff Richard 8. Rose Royce 9. Rolling Stones 10. Shabba Ranks

QUIZ THREE

General

1. Who acquired the nickname of 'The Bardot of Rock' during a tour of Germany in 1982?

2. Who appeared in the TV shows *The Sullivans*, *The Hendersons* and *The Zoo Family* before becoming a pop superstar?

3. Which song a hit for Zager & Evans in 1969 could possibly be a hit 556 years later?

4. Who was the second woman to sing a James Bond theme?

5. Which US group, whose biggest hit came courtesy of the 1980 song 'Babe', named themselves after a mythological river?

6. Which pop star played an outlaw called Candy in the 1971 spaghetti western *Blindman*?

7. Who was arrested in the Will Rogers Memorial Park on April 7, 1998?

8. Which of the following was the original name of The Who, was it, The Odd Numbers, The Even Numbers, The High Numbers, The Low Numbers or The Prime Numbers?

9. Which punk rocker chronicled his time in Pentonville Jail in a book entitled *Inside Information*?

10. Who played Ike Turner in the film *What's Love Got to do With it*?

ANSWERS
1. Kim Wilde 2. Kylie Minogue 3. 'In The Year 2525' 4. Nancy Sinatra 5. Styx 6. Ringo Starr 7. George Michael 8. The High Numbers 9. Hugh Cornwell of the Stranglers 10. Laurence Fishburne

QUIZ FOUR

A tasty round

1. David Gates, James Griffin, Mike Botts and Robb Royer are the four members of which pop group?

2. Which song has been a hit for The Tarriers, Shirley Bassey and Harry Belafonte?

3. What is the nationality of the progressive rock group Tangerine Dream?

4. Which film features the song 'The Night They Invented Champagne'?

5. Which act won the Eurovision Song Contest for Israel in 1979 with the song 'Hallelujah'?

6. 'Echo Beach' was the biggest hit for which Canadian group?

7. What is the name of the memorial in Central Park, New York dedicated to John Lennon?

8. Which Manchester band recorded the album *Meat is Murder* in 1984?

9. Which Elvis Costello song contains the line, "and a lip print on a half filled cup of coffee"?

10. Which song connects Neil Diamond, UB 40 and Tony Tribe?

ANSWERS

1. Bread 2. 'The Banana Boat Song' 3. German 4. *Gigi* 5. Milk and Honey 6. Martha and The Muffins 7. Strawberry Fields 8. The Smiths 9. 'A Good Year for the Roses' 10. 'Red Red Wine'; Diamond wrote it, Tony Tribe and UB 40 charted with the song

QUIZ FIVE

General

1. 'Ordinary Lives', 'Still Waters' and 'Lonely Days' were minor hits for which famous pop trio?

2. Which two songs were hits for Eddie Cochran in 1959 and for the Sex Pistols in 1979?

3. What is the surname of the brothers in the 1960s music trio The Bachelors?

4. To whom did guitarist Tommy Allsup give his aeroplane seat on a flight that took off on February 3, 1959?

5. Which singer provided vocals on the Oscar winning songs 'It Goes Like it Goes', 'Up Where we Belong' and 'I've Had the Time of my Life'?

6. Who sang the first line on the 1984 Band Aid hit 'Do They Know It's Christmas'?

7. Who sang the first line on the 1985 USA For Africa hit 'We are the World'?

8. In 1960, The Beatles failed an audition to become which singer's backing band?

9. Which song connects the film *Promises Promises* and the singer Bobbie Gentry?

10. Who provided lead vocals on the Python Lee Jackson hit 'In a Broken Dream'?

QUIZ SIX

Can you identify the songs from their lyrics?
They all include a form of transport in the title...

1. "So we sailed into the sun till we found the sea of green"

2. "I don't believe in Peter Pan, Frankenstein or Superman"

3. "I bought it at Primrose Hill from a bloke in Brazil"

4. "LA proved too much for the man"

5. "I say, 'Please share my umbrella'"

6. "The first mate he got drunk and broke in the Cap'n' trunk"

7. "I thought the only lonely place was on the moon"

8. "You looked so pretty as you were ridin' along"

9. "My brothers and sisters are all aboard, hallelujah"

10. "Mars ain't the kind of place to raise your kids"

ANSWERS
1. 'Yellow Submarine' 2. 'Bicycle Races' 3. 'Driving In My Car' 4. 'Midnight Train to Georgia' 5. 'Bus Stop' 6. 'Sloop John B' 7. 'Jet' 8. 'The Pushbike Song' 9. 'Michael Row The Boat Ashore' 10. 'Rocket Man'

QUIZ SEVEN

1. What is the English translation of the opera title *Il Travatore*?

2. Which pop star, as a child actor played Corky in the TV series *Circus Boy*?

3. Which famous name in the world of pop died in a skiing accident on January 5, 1998?

4. Which song featured in the film *Breakfast at Tiffany's* and went on to become a No 1 hit for Danny Williams?

5. Which group backed Dexy's Midnight Runners on their hit record 'Come on Eileen'?

6. What nationality are the pop group The Cardigans?

7. Who gave up a career in boxing after breaking his nose and released his debut album *Cold Spring Harbor* in 1972?

8. Which chart topping star of the 1960s lost her battle against cancer in March 1999?

9. Which song, first released in November 1957, eventually reached No 1 in December 1986?

10. On which 1985 No 1 hit did Ringo Starr perform with his son Zac?

QUIZ EIGHT

Record labels

1. Which record label founded in 1947 has recorded music by such artists as Ray Charles, Yes, AC DC and The Rolling Stones?

2. Which record labels headquarters is located at 1290, Sixth Avenue, New York?

3. Which label was formed by Chris Blackwell in 1957?

4. Who was appointed head of Parlephone Records in 1955?

5. Which record label was founded by Herb Alpert and Jerry Moss in 1962?

6. On which legendary record label did Johnny Cash, Elvis Presley and Carl Perkins all record?

7. On which label did Abba record all their No 1 hits?

8. On which label did the Bee Gees have their first hit in the UK?

9. Who is the famous partner of Nik Powell who co-founded a record label with him in 1972?

10. On which record label was the first No 1 hit recorded?

QUIZ NINE

....

General

1. Who connects the punk rock groups Adam and the Ants, The Sex Pistols and Bow Wow Wow?

2. Who sang a duet with Kylie Minogue on the record 'Where the Wild Roses Grow'?

3. What does MOBO stand for with regard to the MOBO Awards?

4. In his early career who performed with the groups The King Bees, The Lower Third and The Mannish Boys before embarking on a hugely successful solo career?

5. In what was Eddie Cochran travelling when he died in a road accident?

6. Which song originally released by The Hollies in 1979 became a No 1 hit in 1988 after featuring in a beer TV advert?

7. Who played the piano on the Cat Stevens hit 'Morning has Broken'?

8. The Village People were formed as a tribute to which gay district of New York?

9. Which song-writing duo wrote the hit 'Locomotion' for their babysitter Little Eva?

10. Whose 1969 debut album, *Post Card,* was produced by Paul McCartney?

QUIZ TEN

Can you identify the artists who recorded these farewell songs?

1. 1983   'The Last Film'
2. 1982   'Say Hello Wave Goodbye'
3. 1978   'Goodbye Girl'
4. 1962   'Last Night Was Made for Love'
5. 1970   'Farewell is a Lonely Sound'
6. 1989   'Last of the Famous International Playboys'
7. 1978   'Last Night A DJ Saved My Life'
8. 1970   'Goodbye Sam Hello Samantha'
9. 1985   'The Last Kiss'
10. 1952   'Auf Weidersehn Pet'

ANSWERS
1. Kissing the Pink 2. Soft Cell 3. Squeeze 4. Billy Fury 5. Jimmy Ruffin 6. Morrissey 7. In Deep 8. Cliff Richard 9. David Cassidy 10. Vera Lynn